Copyright © 2019 Rainey Leigh Seraphine, Wizzenhill Publishing

All rights reserved. Without limiting the rights under copyright reserved above, no part of this work/publication may be reproduced, stored in or introduced into a retrieval system, or transmitted, in any form or by any means (electronic, mechanical, print, photocopying, recording or otherwise), without the prior written permission of the copyright owner.

Images retrieved from Pixabay.com. A huge thank you to the wonderful artists who donate their work for free commercial use. Without you, this and all other books by the author would not exist.

ISBN 978-0-6483614-9-7

For Dhani, Astrid and Tahlei

Where is the Easter Bunny?

It is Easter morning
and a bright yellow sun is rising.

Eggs are in the backyard,
but I cannot see the Easter bunny.

Eggs are in the front yard.
Can you see a bunny anywhere?

Here are some more eggs.
Someone has painted flowers on them.
I wonder if it was the Easter bunny?

I can see eggs under the tulips,
but I still cannot see a bunny. Can you?

There are three eggs and three flower bulbs,
but I wish we could see the Easter bunny.
Do you?

Wait! Is that the Easter bunny?
Oh! No, it is a butterfly.

These eggs and tulips are pretty, but where is the bunny?

While we wait for the bunny, can you point to which egg you like best?

Can you count how many eggs there are?
Let's count together?
1 2 3 4 5 6 7 8
There are eight pretty eggs.

Here is a paintbrush.
Have you ever painted an egg?
You're best to have it hard boiled first,
just in case you drop it.

It looks like these eggs are hiding. I wonder if the Easter bunny is hiding too?

Even the painted pig
in the flowery meadow is searching.
She has a smile on her face.
I wonder if she spotted the bunny?

Oh! I can see bunny ears.
Can you see them too?

Is this the Easter bunny?

Now there is another bunny.
"Excuse me," says a cat.
"Are you the Easter bunny?"
The bunny says yes, but she is one of many.

There are lots of Easter bunnies delivering eggs all around the world.

Do you have a bunny like this one?
Is it your special Easter bunny?
His green cardigan matches the grass.

I like his blue cardigan.
It matches the sky.

It looks like this bunny
has been painting her eggs. One is purple,
one is red. One is orange and the other is blue.

The sun is going down now and the Easter bunnies have gone. Perhaps they are going to sleep?

"It's time for me to go to sleep too.
I am glad you found me," says the Easter bunny.
"I wish you, and all the special people in your life,
a very happy Easter."

Other children's picture books by Rainey Leigh Seraphine:

Wicky the Wacky Witch & Grumpy Mr Whilloby
We're Off to the Moon in My Hot Air Balloon
Miranda Merbaby's Mystical World
The Snowflake Who Wouldn't Fall
The Fairies Tale
Bronte's Book
Our Dad Hates Bugs
Theo's World
Bonny Bilby
Skiddy Squirrel's Poetically Preposterous Account
of Awesome Animal Antics

are available at all online bookstores and retail outlets.
Visit: www.raineyleighseraphine.com
or authors Facebook page: raineyleighseraphine

www.ingramcontent.com/pod-product-compliance
Lightning Source LLC
Chambersburg PA
CBHW042145290426
44110CB00002B/118